Gilgamesh's Snake and Other Poems

Middle East Literature in Translation

Michael Beard and Adnan Haydar, *Series Editors*

KING FAHD CENTER
FOR MIDDLE EAST STUDIES

TRANSLATION OF ARABIC LITERATURE
2015 AWARD WINNER

Syracuse University Press and the King Fahd Center for Middle East Studies, University of Arkansas, are pleased to announce GILGAMESH'S SNAKE AND OTHER POEMS as the 2015 winner of the King Fahd Center for Middle East Studies Translation of Arabic Literature Award.

GILGAMESH'S
SNAKE
AND OTHER POEMS

GHAREEB ISKANDER

Translated from the Arabic by
John Glenday and Ghareeb Iskander

BILINGUAL EDITION

Syracuse University Press

An early version of section 2 of "Gilgamesh's Snake" was first published by the Enheduanna Society on www.zipang.org.uk.

Section 1, part of section 4, and section 5 of "Gilgamesh's Snake" were previously published in *This Room Is Waiting: Poems from Iraq and Britain*, edited by Lauren Pyott and Ryan Van Winkle (Glasgow: Freight Books, 2014).

ISBN: 978-0-8156-1071-7 (paperback)   978-0-8156-5374-5 (e-book)

Library of Congress Cataloging-in-Publication Data
Names: Iskandar, Gharīb, 1966– author. | Glenday, John, translator. | Iskandar, Gharīb, 1966– Poems. Selections. English. | Iskandar, Gharīb, 1966– Poems. Selections.
Title: Gilgamesh's snake and other poems : bilingual edition / Ghareeb Iskander ; translated from the Arabic by John Glenday and Ghareeb Iskander.
Description: First edition. | Syracuse : Syracuse University Press, 2016. | Series: Middle East literature in translation | In English and Arabic.
Identifiers: LCCN 2015048634| ISBN 9780815610717 (pbk. : alk. paper) | ISBN 9780815653745 (e-book)
Classification: LCC PJ7938.S45 A2 2016 | DDC 892.7/17–dc23
LC record available at http://lccn.loc.gov/2015048634

Contents

Gilgamesh's Snake and Other Poems

أفعى كَلكَامش

Gilgamesh's Snake

I. أغنيـة

غنّى كلَّ شيء:
غنى الأرصفة النائمة
والفجر الغريب.
غنى روحه وجسده.
حبيبته وأمه
غنى الملائكة والشياطين.

غنى الربيع -
الأزهار التي تنمو
من بعد ليل طويل.
غنى الشوارع
لم يغن الجدران.

غنى
وغنى
وغنى.

غنى بعينيه
وبيديه
وبقلبه
لم يغن بفمه.
كان صمته أبلغ أغنية.

كانت حياته
رقصة موت
وأيامه
فراغاً هامساً.

4

I. Song

He sang the sum of things:
the drowsing pavement,
the unfamiliar dawn.
He sang his soul and body.
His lover and his mother.
He sang angels, he sang devils.

He sang springtime—
the flowers that open themselves
after a long night.
He sang the streets
but he wouldn't sing the hindering walls.

He sang
and he sang
and sang.

He sang with his eyes
and with his hands.
He sang with his heart
but his mouth did no singing.
The richest of all his songs was silence.

His life was
death's little dance
and his days all
emptiness—a whispering void.

II. البداية المفقودة

أيها السيد
لا تؤرخ للعدم
لا تقل جاء من جاء
وذهب من ذهب
لا تكشف عن الخلود
هويتك الباهتة.
لقد كنت فيما مضى تنعم بالمسميات
بعبارات الطاعة
وبهلوان الكلام.
أما اليوم،
فليس أمامك سوى أن تنجو
وترحل الى عتمة ثانية.

هذا هو الحل:
أن تسطع بما ليس لك
أن تبارك النهايات
أن تقول: لا وجود هناك.

أنا كنت هنا
وأنت كنت هناك.
كلانا تشفع بموته.
كلانا أمر الفجر
بالانزواء.

أيها السيد
لا تقل ذهب الجميع الى المقبرة
هذه الصحراء التي تراها
كانت فينا أولاً
لم نكن نسمع صوت الريح
لم نكن نلمس الرمل
كنا نلوذ فقط بالشجرة القديمة
بالأماني التي تتكوم مثلَ ليْل.

II. The Lost Beginning

Master!
Don't write histories for no reason.
Don't talk about someone arriving
and someone else going away.
Don't let anyone glimpse that white shadow
called Eternity, which you cast.
Long ago you loved the names for things,
the rules of grammar and
wordplay.
Today, however,
your only choice is to carry on
so that you may set out for life's second darkness.

Here's the answer:
Shine with a light that does not belong to you.
Bless endings.
Say, there is no such thing as existence.

I was here.
You were there.
We both intervened in our own deaths.
We both told the dawn light
to keep its head down.

Master!
Don't say they're all in the graveyard.
You see this desert all around you?
First of all, it grew inside us.
At first we couldn't hear the voice of the wind
or run our fingers through the sand.
We could only bow down to the old tree
to the desires, which grew like dark fruit in the night.

ماذا يقول هذا الذي يقف خلفي؟
لم يقل شيئاً
كان يردد أغاني هجرناها
عندما عبرنا الطريق الى ضفة ثانية.

لا تقل ذهب الجميع
أنتَ فقط من أراد الرحيل
من سماء الوهم الى سماء الوهم.

أ لم تكن في سباتك تزهو؟

لا تتكلم عن الأرض
تكلم عن البهاء الذي ينمو قرب هاوية
ويموت قرب امرأة
قالت لي ذات ليلة ماطرة:
لم تستهوني الدمعة
لم يستهوني الفم الذي ينشج
ولا العين التي تذرف.

ها قد أصابتك المحنة الأزلية
ما هو لون الموت إذن؟
وما هو لون الحياة؟

إما أن تقول نعم نعم نعم
للغياب كله
او تقول لا لا لا
للحضور كله
هذه هي صرختك الأخيرة:
ماتت الأفعى.

لقد خسرنا الوجود
وخسرنا العدم
لقد ضاع كل شيء:

What is that person standing behind me saying?
He said nothing.
He was just singing our forgotten songs
as we set out on our travels to the other side.

Don't say everyone has gone.
You were the only one who wanted to go
from the false sky to the counterfeit sky.

Were you not once proud of your long sleep?

Don't talk about the world,
talk about the beauty that grows on the cliff edge
and dies inside a woman.
On a rainy night she turned to me and said,
The crying didn't impress me.
The weeping mouth, didn't impress me.
The eye that shed the tears didn't impress me either.

Now you are struck down with the sickness that never resolves.
Tell me, what color is death?
And what color is life, for that matter?

You're either nodding at
all those absences
or shaking your head
at everything that's really there.
And the very last thing you'll shout out is,
The snake is dead.

We misplaced life
and we can't find it's opposite
so everything is lost to us:

ضاعت النهاية
وضاعت البداية.

أيها السيد
لا تبحث عن الأبدية.
لقد سبقك اليها رﺑﻴﺐ القلق،
جدُّنا كَلكَامش
انعم بالنهر الذي يجري دماً
وبالعين التي تجري دمعاً.
انعم بالنهاية
ببرودة القبر
بالوحشة التي تمجدها الغربان
لا تتكلم عن أهمية أن تكون وحيداً
لقد سبقوك اليها
بمطارقهم وأمانيهم الموجعة.

لماذا لا تقول الحقيقة؟
لماذا لا تشير الى المعنى
كل المعنى؟
لماذا لا تقول إن الجدار الذي أقمناه
كان هشاً للغاية؟

غرف مليئة بأسمال الموتى
هذا هو وطني
موسيقى الخراب
نواح لم نألفه من قبل
أحضان كثيرة
قديمة وجديدة:
لصوص
قوادون
سماسرة
عسكريون
نخاسون
بائعو شعارات.

the end is lost
and the beginning is lost.

Master!
Don't search for everlasting life.
Our grandfather, Gilgamesh,
who was born in sadness, went there before you,
waded through the river flowing with blood
delighted in the eye that flows with tears.
Love the ending of things,
the chill of the grave
the strangeness the ravens sing of.
Don't prattle on about needing to be alone.
They all went there long before you
following the ache and beat of their desires.

Just tell the truth.
Tell us what it means,
exactly what it means.
Why don't you just say the wall we built
was shoddy, to say the least?

A series of rooms filled to overflowing with rags taken from
      the dead,
that's what my country is—
the music of misery and destruction.
Once upon a time, it wouldn't have been recognized.
Many factions: both old and new
Thieves
Pimps
Wheeler-dealers
Gun-runners
Slave traders
Sloganmongers.

لا تتكلم عن الحنين.
لا تتكلم عن البلاد التي رحلت
والبلاد التي احترقت.
لا تتكلم
عن الوجد.
تكلم فقط عن الشجرة
واصطفافها الطويل.
عن عتبة الروح
عن أمجاد خرساء.
تكلم عني،
أنا الأعمى،
لم أرَ كلَّ شيء
رأيت فقط الالوانَ التي تشيرُ الى الألم.

Don't talk about longing.
Don't talk about the nation we lost
and the nation that was consumed in fire.
Don't talk about love.
Just talk about the tree
and its long shadow.
Talk about the doorstep of the soul,
and unsung glories.
Talk about me,
the Blind Man,
who saw nothing,
only the colors that are shed
that show the way to where pain lies.

III. شيء ما بدأ يتكلم

إلــى أبــي

بدأت هدأة المعنى
بدأت المسرة
شيء ما بدأ يتكلم
في الأعين المتحجرة.

بدأ التوهج
بدأ العنفوان
بدأ الغياب
الغياب الأخير للكلمة.
لا أعني غيابَكِ
لا أعني الماضي.
طريق واحد فقط
هو العمر.
حياة واحدة
وغيابات شتى ـ
بحجم الكلمةِ
بحجم معناكِ
وأنت تتسلقين معي
جسدَ الكتابة.

لم تسعفكِ الكلمة
لم يسعفكِ المعنى
فقط قلق الأب
وهو يغني
فقط صوته
فقط كلمته الأخيرة
عيناه وهو يبتسم

III. Something Began to Talk

To my father

All meaning was put on hold.
Happiness came back—
something began to talk
behind eyes that were once twin pebbles.

A certain brilliance opened itself
and strength rose up
and all absences flowered
and the most recent was language.
Mother, I don't mean your absence,
I don't mean the past.
Growing old
isn't the only way.
It's your life,
but such a range of things are lost—
the breadth of the word
the altitude of meaning
as alongside me you scale
the sheer face of literature.

Language has never sheltered you,
meaning has never come to your aid.
Mother, it is only Father's regard helps you.
When he sings,
his voice alone
or his final words.
His eyes whenever he smiles.

فقط عمره:
أوهامه وأحلامه
أفراحه التي لم ترَ الضوء
شجونه
قنديله الأخير
دموعه التي تطفو على أسطح الذاكرة.

لم يكن يسعى الى الكمال
كان يتشبه فقط بالوردة
بالشجرة الأم، بأوراقها
بجدل الطبيعة
صباح أزرق كالبحر
وليل مضيء كالأمل.

شاهدة جديدة
هذا النهار
شاهدة جديدة
لم تمحُ الأمطار بعدُ تواريخها
فهل احتاج الى قنديل نار؟
ليس الضوء
ليس الموسيقى التي تنبع من رحم الكلمة.

لقد كُنْتَهُ يوماً ما
ذلك البعيد
ذلك الذي يتجذر بالحلم
لقد كُنْتَهُ في مجده
الذي تضيق به الحكمة.

صماء هذه الحروف
بينما كلماتك
أوسع من تاريخ مدو

His life alone:
>   his fantasies, his dreams
>   his hidden joys
>   his sadnesses
>   his last light
>   his tears suspended from memory's gable.

He didn't set out to be perfect,
he just did as the rose does;
he did as the leaf of the old tree does.
The search for truth in Nature
is like daylight, blue as an open sea;
it's like a star-shaken night, shimmering with hope.

It's a fresh gravestone
with the day carved into it.
A new gravestone
so the rain hasn't worn away its dates.
Do I need an open flame?
No, no light,
not that music born out of language.

Once upon a time I was
the thousand-mile man, the one
dreams are always taking root in.
I was him in all his glory,
his wisdom withering away.

Language has no voice,
but your words
are louder than the roar of history.

ليست الرؤيا   وليس الأمل الكاذب.
وبالطبع
ليس هذا الحجر الذي تتحدث عنه
وليست أيام الغياب
إنه التلاشي
التلاشي الأخير
للكلمة
السواد الذي رفعناه معاً
دمعنا الذي تحجر
في الانتظار
في الأمل
في الأكاذيب الكثيرة.
لم تكن نوحاً
ولم تكن العشبة
لقد كنتَ البداية التي لا تنتهي:

أجراس الولادة
وأجراس الموت معاً

موسيقى غياباتك المتعددة
ولا سفح أخضر لكَ

لا سكينة لآمالك المستحيلة
لا أنهار لعطشك الدائم
ولا حتى سراب
صحراء فقط هي أحلامك
غياب يبتدئ وينتهي بك
بموتك وحياتك
هذه هي لعبة الكلمة
طين الغياب.

لم يقل إنني ولدت
كان يحتضرُ كلَّ أيامه

It's neither vision nor hopeless hope.
And, of course
it's not the stone you are talking about,
not the days of absence,
it's the disappearance
the last disappearance
of the word,
of the darkness we have raised together,
of our tears that congeal
in the waiting,
in the hope,
in many lies.
you were neither Noah
nor the grass,
you were a beginning that has no end:

the birth chimes
and the funeral bells

you were the music of your countless absences
and there are no lush foothills for you.

No calmness for your impossible hopes,
no rivers for your permanent thirst,
not even a mirage.
Your dreams are nothing but a desert,
an absence begun and ended by you,
by your death and your life.
This is the game of the word,
the soil of the absence.

He did not say I was born.
He was dying all his days,

كلَّ سنينه
كلَّ أحلامه
لم يقل هذا الرجل الصامت شيئاً
كعادته.
لم يتكلم،
فقط أشار الى وديعته
الى أعلام سود؛
مجده الغابر
لم يقل هؤلاء أبنائي
كان يسميهم فقط.

هكذا ينتهي كلُ شيء.
معنى الزهرة التي تنمو بعيدة عن الغصن
فتكشف النهايات
عن حكايا الخراب الأخير
حيث تركته هناك وحيداً
قرب موته
يسمو على كذبة الحياة الوحيدة؛

الخرافة التي تقول:
-    مَن أنت؟
-    ما هذه المودة المستحيلة؟
فحتى الروح
حتى الأشجار التي كانت تعلو
أصبحت جرداء
حتى القناديل الكبيرة
التي لعبنا قبالتها
أيام طفولتنا.

فهل تذكر الماضي
ذلك الذي سرق الأغنية؟
هل تذكر خروجي معك
في نزهة الألم؟

all his years,
all his dreams.
The silent man did not say anything—
that was his habit.
He did not speak;
he only pointed to his hopes,
to black flags,
his bygone glory.
He did not say these are my children,
he only named them.

Therefore, everything ends.
The meaning of the flower that grows far from its branch
so that the endings reveal
more tales of the last devastation
where I left him alone
near death.
He climbs on the only lie of life—

the myth that says,
—Who are you?
—What is this impossible affection?
then even the soul
even the trees that were growing
became barren.
Even the great lanterns
before which we played
in the days of our childhood.

Do you remember the past
that stole the song?
Do you remember me when I came out with you
for the journey of the agony?

فلِمَ لم تحدثْني عن عوارض الجسد
التي كانت تنمو قرب الروح؟
كانت كلماتك فقط عن تلك الليلة
عن غابة آمال
عن ألم قديم.
قدر يعود ثانية.
ليست القصيدة إياها
ولا المرأة التي حدثتك عنها.

إنه الألم،
الألم نفسه
الغياب الذي عشناه معاً
سواقي الطفولة اليابسة.

كان مثله تماماً
مثل كَلكَامش
يستحم بالشمس
يشرب دمعه من كأس
لكنه
لم ير الأرز،
لم ير أي شيء
رأى فقط كثبان الفجيعة؛
رأى الغياب
في فتنته الآسرة.

So why did you not tell me about the barriers of the body
that had been growing close to the soul?
Your words were only about that night
about a forest of hopes
about an old pain.
Destiny returns again.
It's not the same poem,
nor the woman that I told you about.

It's a pain,
the same pain,
the absence we experienced together,
the dry waterways of childhood.

He was just like him,
like Gilgamesh.
Bathe by the sun.
Drink his tears from a cup.
But
he did not see the cedars,
he did not see anything
but the dunes of bereavement,
the absence
in its captivating charm.

IV. كيف يمكن لي أن أدونه؟

أيها السيد
ماذا سأفعل بهذا الخراب؟
كيف يمكن لي أن أدونه؟
كيف أمرّ عليه؟
أيُّ جسرٍ هذا الذي يحملني الى المتاهة؟
كل شيءٍ احترق.
كل شيء في مهب الحقيقة
أو مهب الفراغ
كل شيء -
حتى الأفعى.
لم تعد شاهدة عليه،
لا يعنيها الأمر بعد الآن.
لا يعنيها أن تكون عنقاء؛
تريد أن تنطفئ فقط
تتلاشى
تتلاشى
الى أن تصير رماداً.
فلم تعد تفهم كوابيسها القديمة،
المسرات الذابلة والأحزان الكبيرة.
والأوجاع ...
(الحكمة التي لا تنضب أبداً)
أ تذكرينها ...؟
عادت هذه المرة
بثوب جديد
لكنها هي نفسها:

الغيابات القديمة
والأماني التي بلون الرماد.

أيها السيد
لا أنهار في أرضك
لا ماء يروي عطشك القديم،

24

IV. How Will I Ever Write about It?

Master!
What's to be done with this devastation?
How will I ever write about it?
How can I possibly move beyond it?
What sort of path led me to this labyrinth?
Everything is razed to the ground.
The truth, that whirlwind, blew it all away,
sent it tumbling downwind towards oblivion.
Everything vanished—
even the Snake.
It no longer notices what's going on,
no longer cares.
It has no desire to transform into a Phoenix;
all it wants is to be snuffed out,
to fade away,
and so it withers
into windblown ash.
It no longer understands the old nightmares,
those withered joys and unfathomable sorrows.
And the agonies . . .
(a knowledge that never heals)
. . . do you remember them?
This time they came back
in a new guise,
but they are always the same:

all those old losses
and longings colored like ash.

Master!
There are no rivers in your country
no water to quench your terrible thirst,

صحراء فقط تمتد فينا
لا ضوء
في هذه العتمة.

أمل كاذب هذا الذي تراه امامك،
وهم
لا ...
ليس حلماً
لا ...
لا تغنِّ.
لا صوت فيها
هذه المدينة
أشباح فقط.
كل شيء احترق
يحترق ... يحترق
هذه الأرض
غابة من لهب
لم ترَ النور
ولن ترى الضحكة فيها.

كَلكَامش
وحيد الآن
يغطيه الثلج
يتقاسمه الموج
تلفه الحشائش
يستنجد بالعشب
لكن
لا أحد هناك يسمعه.
فأوروك خاوية،
لا أحد فيها
يلفها الصمت.
شوارعها خاوية
يمشي فيها وحيداً -

there is only the great desert, reaching out into us.
No glimmer of light
in all that acreage of dark.

What you see before you is a forlorn hope,
a will-o'-the-wisp,
but no,
not a dream
no . . .
Don't even try to sing.
This city should have no voice,
only ghosts.
Everything was burned
and everything is still burning,
always burning.
This entire country
is a forest in flames
and you will not glimpse a single thread of light in it,
and you will never laugh again.

Gilgamesh.
He's alone now.
Snow covers him.
He's all at sea.
Swaddled in lushness,
he looks to the grass of life for help
but there's no one there
to hear him.
Uruk is an empty ruin,
all its people fled.
Such devastation; the streets
shimmer in a caul of silence.
He wanders alone—

لا أشجار تستظل بها روحه الهائمة
لا كأس تطفئ غربته.
يبكي وحيداً
ولأن انتصاره كان هزيمة دائمة
ظل طوال عمره
يمتطي سعفة من نخيل.

يمشي في شوارع أوروك
يقابل اناساً غرباء
سحنتهم سحنته
أسماؤهم تشبه اسمه
لكنهم غرباء
غرباء
في هذه البلاد الغريبة.

أيها السيد
يحرقني هذا الضوء؛
هذه الموسيقى القادمة
من آفاق الروح
يحرقني هذا الأمل الكاذب
هذا الجسد الذي يحترق
هذه المرايا التي لا تشير الى شيء
تحرقني هذه العتمة
لا شيء هناك
لا شيء
ارحلْ عنها
لا تعد اليها
ربما لا تنتهي هذه القصيدة
لكن عليّ أن اختار بين وهمين:
حياتين أو موتين
عليَّ أن اختار بين أمرين
بين عذابين
كلاهما مر!

not a single tree shades his scorched soul,
no wine to quench his longing.
All alone, he cries,
and because victory for him is a defeat that never ends
till the ends of his life, he must
ride the magic palm frond.

He walks the streets of Uruk,
meets strangers
who look like him,
their names like his name,
but they are strangers.
Strangers
in this unrecognizable land.

Master!
This light burns through me;
this swelling music from the fringes of the soul
always growing closer.
I am burned by the lies Hope told me.
This body, burning
these mirrors reflecting absolutely nothing.
Even the darkness burns.
There is nothing there,
not a thing.
Get yourself away from here.
Don't ever come back.
Perhaps this is a poem that never ends.
But I must choose between two illusions:
two existences, two deaths.
I must decide between them,
these two agonies
each filled with its own particular pain!

حلمتُ بأنني في غابات الأرز
أقاتل نفسي.
أنا خمبابا
الحارس الأمين للحكمة الجديدة.

ممالك تتهاوى،
وأخرى تقوم
وأنا هنا
بانتظار الهزيمة،
بانتظار الحكمة التي لا تأتي.

هذه المدينة موت.
نهارها دم،
وليلها سواد.
على أوراق كثيرة كتبتُ هذه القصيدة؛
أوراق الأمل،
أوراق اليأس.
على البحر واليابسة،
كتبتُ هذه القصيدة
عن الحب ونقيضه.

هذه هي قصيدتي،
بيضاء بلون الكفن
خضراء بلون الدمع.

سأكتب حكمتي على الماء.
سأقول فيها
ما خبأته الأعين
وما رواه النسيان.
سأدون الضحكة الغائبة.
هذا أنا:
رائي الودائع الزائلة.

I once dreamed I was deep in the cedar forests
battling against myself.
I had become Humbaba
guardian of the new wisdom.

Kingdoms fall,
others rise up
but all the while I linger on
waiting for defeat to find me,
waiting for the wisdom that will never come.

This city is the city of death.
Its daylight is stained with blood,
its night, an utter dark.
I wrote down this poem on a thousand blank pages:
pages of hope,
pages of despair.
Far out to sea and far from the sea,
on a thousand sheets of paper
I wrote about love, and the opposite of love.

This is the poem I inscribed,
as white as the whitest shroud,
as green as shed tears.

I will engrave my wisdom on pages of water.
It will describe
everything the eyes concealed
and all the stories oblivion whispered to me.
I will write down the vanished laughter.
This is what I am:
I am the shaman of momentary faith.

V. خاتمة

لم يكن قد رأى
أي شيء
كانت النهاية فقط
ما يُحيط به:

لا أبراج
لا سلالم
ولا حتى أغنية
يغنيها في تلك الوحشة.

حلق عالياً
وبعدما أصبح قاب قوسين
أو أدنى من أحلامه البعيدة
تدلى
بقوة
نحو
القصيدة.

V. Conclusion

He had seen
nothing;
all around him
the ending of things, nothing more:

no towers
no stairways,
there wasn't even a song
to sing in all that desolation.

He was soaring high; so very high
he was pulled close
to his uttermost dreams
and suddenly tumbled back down,
plummeted
towards
the poem.

كتاب الصمت

The Book of Silence

1

ليس الحب،
ولا حتى الدمع،
ليست عينيكِ،
ولا حتى رموشكِ التي تَكَحّلت بالأرق.
ليس الغياب،
ولا حتى الصدى الذي ظل يرن في الذاكرة.
ليس الليل
وليس النهار
بالطبع
ليس كلّ ذلك.

الموت وحدَهُ
سيد الأسئلة
وسيد الأجوبة.
له الكلمة العليا،
يتمتم أسماءنا
واحداً واحداً
يا لقسوته!
كيف
مر عليكِ
في تلك الليلة الباردة؟

2

بين عمائين
نقف الآن حيارى،
بين اللحظة التي يسمونها وجوداً
واللحظة التي يسمونها موتاً.
مَن كان الأوّل يا ترى؟

1

Not love,
not even tears,
not your eyes,
nor even your eyelashes dark with sleeplessness.
Not absence,
not even its echo, resonating in my memory.
Not the night
and not the day,
it's none of that
of course.

Only Death
is the question master
and holds all the answers.
Death has the last word,
muttering our names
one after the other.
How heartless it is!
How
did it walk by you
that cold night?

2

We stand here baffled
between two blindnesses:
between the moment called existence
and the moment called death.
Which came first?

الوهم الذي يتسلقنا كالأزل،
أم الحلم الذي يكتبنا ورقة.. ورقة
لكن الهدهد
الذي ليس له سوى أن لا يأتي
لم يُنبئنا بشيء -
ليس خوفاً من جبروت الملك
مع أن المَنْسأة لم تقع بعد
بقيت في يده
وبقي هو واقفاً
ربما رأفة بالجمال
ذلك الذي له سطوة الصمت.

3

مَن جاءنا بنبأ الخيبة؟
كيف ضعنا كلَّ تلك السنين؟
مَن قادنا الى هذه المتاهة
الى هذه المخاضة من الدمع؟

ألبوم الصور القديمة،
دراجة الأسى،
الخسارات التي لا نهاية لها
وأحلام البيت الجديد
الذي انتهى الى محل حلاقة!

البحار التي عبرناها مسرعين
نحو النهاية
أو نحو الأمل.
الصداقات المتقطعة كأعمارنا؛
ليلنا الطويل البارد،
حكايات الشوق
وقصص الذين يذهبون
ولا يعودون.

The illusion of eternity that condenses in us,
or the dream that writes us, page by page.
But the Hoopoe
whose only choice was absence
predicted nothing—
not out of fear of the king's wrath,
although he still grasped the scepter
safe in his hand
and stood firm
stunned by beauty, perhaps,
which has the power to command silence.

3

Who brought us the disappointing news?
How did we lose all those years?
Who led us to the labyrinth,
to that river of tears?

The old photograph album,
the sad bicycle,
the losses that never end,
the wishful dreams of a new home
that turned into a barber's shop!

The seas we raced across
towards a destination
or hope.
Friendships undone, just like our lives,
our endless cold nights,
tales of longing,
stories of the departed
who never return.

غرباء الوطن
والمنافي معاً

يا إلهي
كيف حصل كل هذا؟

4

بين خطين
لا يوصلان الى شيء
تهتُ
ولم يرشدني الغراب.

كان عليّ أن أدفن الحقيقة
والوهم معاً.
كان عليّ أن أذبح الكلمة / الحلم
الذي تبخر، كما يقال،
وترك بين طياته
أملاً كاذباً.

كان وكان..
لكن الخطين اللذين لا يوصلان الى أيما شيء
تاها معي
بانتظار المعجزة!

5

إذن
لستَ أنتَ هو
ولا أنا أنا؛
حياتان تقتربان من العدم،

Strangers to both
home and exile.

My Lord,
how did all these come to be?

4

I was lost
between two parallels
that went nowhere
and the raven couldn't show me the way.

I had to bury both truth
and illusion at the same time.
I had to kill off the word/dream
that evaporated, as they say,
leaving only false hope
in its husk.

I had to . . .
But those lines going nowhere
stayed with me,
waiting for a miracle!

5

So
you are not him
and I am not me;
two lives approaching oblivion,

معنيان مختلفان،
صورتان قديمتان – جديدتان عن الألم.

ذكرى
تغيب وتظهر.
طيف
توهمناه معاً
يلدغ الذاكرة.

عشب جديد - لا...

غيابات شتى هذا العالم
والخسارة واحدة.

6

مَن أنا؟
قال هذا الصوت المرتجف
من أنا؟
من أنا؟
أغنية في الصباح
أم ليلة قاتلة؟

لا ...

أنا أكثر من واحد.
أكثر من صوت
أكثر من شجرة.
أكثر من نهار
وأكثر من ليل
لكن صمتي فريد
لا لون له.

two different meanings,
two personifications of hurt, both old and new.

A memory
hides itself and appears.
We both thought
it was a continuum,
aching in the memory.

New grass—not a blade . . .

How varied are the absences of the world,
but the losses are identical.

6

Who am I?
This voice said, trembling
Who am I?
Who am I?
A song in the morning
or a fatal darkness?

No . . .

I am more than one thing,
more than a voice
and more than a song.
I am more than a day
more than a night
but my silence is unique
and colorless.

7

قلبه
أو الخسران فقط
مَن يُكمل تلك اللوعة
تلك الأغنية.
مروره بدرب الألم وحيداً،
الساقية الصغيرة
التي كان يعبرها
منتظراً غيمة لم تهطل أبداً.

أو الغياب
الذي يسميه حضوراً
سمّه ما شئت:
وجوداً ضائعاً
عمراً معلقاً كبندول ساعة عاطلة.

سمّه الحرب،
أو سمّه الشظية.
سمّه ما شئتَ،
لا شيء أصعب
من تلك الحقيقة الكاذبة!

8

الحروف
التي رددتها شفتاكِ
قبل أناملكِ
كانت بمنتهى الحقيقة
بمنتهى الصمت.

لكن البوح
الذي لا يشبه إلّا نفسه

7

His desire
or his loss alone
finishes that anguish,
    completes that song.
All alone he walked the way of anguish,
    he passed the stream
    he had to cross,
        waiting for a cloud that brought no rain.

Or that absence
Which he calls a presence,
call it what you will:
a wasted life,
a life hanging like the pendulum in a broken clock.

Think of it as war,
think of it as shrapnel.
Call it anything you like,
but there's nothing harder
than that false truth!

8

The letters
that your lips whispered
before your fingertips
were so silent
    and so real.

But the revelation,
which is like nothing else

والذي عشنا أكاذيبه الوارفة،
لا يقوى إلّا على وصفكِ
قدراً يشبه الخسران
قدراً يتيه بكِ
وبأكاذيبه -
التي ظلت معنا
تنتظر
تنتظر
دونما جدوى.

9

أيها اليمّ
الذي يتلاطم فيّ!
أيها الشوق الذي لا حدّ له!
أيها الخوف
الذي عشعش طويلاً!

أيتها الضحكة!
التي أطلقناها معاً.
لم نكن فرحين بها.
كان الدمع، شفيع العزلة،
يتسلقنا بصمت.

10

لا صورة لي في الجبّ
وليس لي إخوة.
لم يعنِي أحدٌ
وليس في رحلتي ما يثير العجب.

whose exaggerated tales we fell for,
it can only describe you
as fate or loss,
a fate undone by you
and by its own lies—
lies that have been waiting with us.
Waiting
and waiting,
but to no purpose.

9

O sea
crashing inside me!
O endless desire!
O fear
that has lodged here too long!

O laughter!
We laughed so much together
that we were made miserable by it
and tears, which are the patron saint of loneliness,
climbed silently through us.

10

There's no reflection of me in the well
and I have no brothers.
No one sold me;
my journey contains no surprises.

أسئلة تقيم ها هنا؛
قربك، قرب نفسك،
لصيقة بك.
- ما هي؟
- لا أعرف!

إنني أثرثر فقط.
اقول ولا أقول،

هذا هو الصمت؛
معناه الذي يسرقنا لحظة بعد لحظة.

11

وحدَه الصمت،
لم يكن ثمة شيء البتة،
رحلة ابتدأنا بها
وسننتهي اليها!
قدرية
ليس لنا سواها .

لكن الصمت،
بهذيانه المعهود،
لا يكف عن استنطاق
الأبدية
التي تتلألأ بها
عيناكِ.

12

تاريخ أعمى
هذه المدينة،

Questions are condensing, here,
all around you,
close beside you.
—What are they?
—I have no idea!

I just babble on.
I speak and I do not speak,

this is what the silence is;
its significance robs us moment by moment.

11

Only silence,
that's all there is,
a journey we have begun
a journey that will be our end!
Resignation,
that's all we have.

But silence,
raving as usual,
will never stop questioning
Eternity
where your eyes brightly
gleam.

12

This city is
a sightless history;

ليست بابل التي تعرفها الذاكرة،
ولا سومر التي طواها النسيان.

تاريخ أعمى -
وليس هناك سوى الموت،
بدمه الذي لا يجف
وبيارقه التي تهتف لنا كل يوم.

ليس هذا كلّ الحكاية.
الرجال الذين حدثتكِ عنهم
عادوا الى اللعبة القديمة؛
لعبة الأمل

تصوري!

لعبة أن نكون
من حيث لا نكون
وليست ثمة مشكلة.

لعبة أن نحلم
ثم يكبر الحلم
يكبرُ ... يكبرُ...

ثم يموت
وحيداً.
-   مَن أنت أم حلمك؟
-   لا أدري وليست ثمة مشكلة!

13 : سفسطة

-   أين أنا الآن؟
-   في هذه البلاد

it's not remembered Babylon,
it's not forgotten Sumer.

A sightless history—
there is only death,
blood, which will not dry,
and its flags that gesture to us day after day.

But this is not the whole story.
The men I mentioned before
have gone back to that old game,
the game called Hope.

Imagine that!

The game of existing
where we do not exist
and there's no problem with that.

It's the dreaming game
and the dream matures,
it grows and grows . . .

and then utterly alone
it dies.
—Is that you or your dream?
—I don't know, and it doesn't matter!

13: Sophistry

—Where am I now?
—In this country

- أي واحدة ؟
- لا أعرف سوى *أنك في البلاد التي أنتَ فيها* .

- ماذا يعني هذا؟
- لا شيء على الاطلاق سوى أنك هنا ولست هناك
- لكن الصمت هو هو؟
- نعم هو هو .

- واللعبة، هي هي ؟
- كلا *ليست هي هي* .

- كيف؟
- *لا أدري*
- ما العمل إذن؟
- *ابحث فيه وعنه* .
- ما هو؟
- *الصمت*
سيجيبك ببلاغته المعهودة!

14

ماذا يفعل هذا الشاعر؟
إنه يقف هناك
قبالة اليأس
محمّلاً بالحلم.
لم يقاتل كدون كيخوته
ولم يعشق كقيس
ولم يسكر كأبي نواس.

كان فقط
يكتب الشعر.

52

—Or that one?
—*I've no idea, but you're in whichever country you are in.*

—What does that mean?
—*It means only that you are here and you are not there.*
—But the silence is the same old silence?
—*Yes, that is so.*

—And the game is the same old game?
—*No. It's not the same.*

—How can that be?
—*I don't know.*
—So what's to be done?
—*Search through it and search for it.*
—But what is it?
—*It is silence*
   and it will answer you with its customary eloquence!

14

What does our poet do?
He stands upright
face-to-face with despair
brimful of dreams.
He doesn't battle like Don Quixote
and he doesn't love like Qays;
he doesn't drink wine like Abu Nawas.

He simply
writes poetry.

يفعل كلّ ذلك
وحده،
ليس من عدة له
سوى الصمت
يدوّن الجروح التي تجري كنهر
والأماني التي أعطبتها السنين.

كان...
وكان...
هذا الشاعر
الذي يسحره غار الصمت
لا غار الكلمات!

15

كم هي جميلة
الأراضي التي وطئتها قدماي
والأماني التي لم يطئها قلبي بعد.

والليالي،
الليالي الطويلة،
والصمت؛
ذلك البوح الشقي
أصبح أغنيتنا الوحيدة!

أما العشب،
فلم يكن اخضراره سوى
لون نهاراتكِ
المضيئة بالأمل.

He always does that
alone;
his only instrument
is the silence
when he notes down wounds that run like rivers
and desires crippled by the passing years.

He writes . . .
and he writes . . .
our poet
enchanted by the laurel of silence
not by the laurel woven from words!

15

How beautiful
those places are where I wandered
and all the desires where I have not yet set foot.

And the nights,
the long nights,
and the silence;
the sad epiphany
that grew into our only song!

As for the grass,
Its lushness was nothing but
the color of your life
lit up by green hope.

16

ثمة فتنة يعرفها قلبي.
ثمة أنهار تتسع له وحده،
ثمة بحار تأتيه في الحلم.
ثمة مدارات
وثمة نسيان كذلك
تنحى تلك اللحظة جانباً
تاركاً العشبة القديمة
ذاكرةً لا تتسع إلا للصمت.

17

أنتِ فقط من له الحق في ترسبات الماضي
أما الحاضر فليس أمامه
سوى الصمت!

صرخة مكبوتة،
إذن كانت تلك الموسيقى.
لن أكتب عنها أي شيء.
لن أقول: إن الزمن الذي سرقناه معاً
قد أضعناه معاً.

لن أقول: احترقت سنواتنا
كالضوء!
لن أقول: أنتِ فراشة العمر
لا رفيف سوى
الليل
ترتوي منه
عزلتنا المضيئة!

16

My heart knows temptation.
There are rivers that flow nowhere else,
there are seas that in dreams crash against it.
Moons drift over it; and in that place for that moment
forgetfulness stepped aside
abandoning to the old grass
a memory just wide enough
for silence and nothing else.

17

Only you may gather the Past's harvests
and the Present holds no promise
but silence!

A cry was stifled,
the music, hushed.
I will write nothing about it.
I will not say: Those stolen hours we spent together,
                  we lost together.

I will not say: Our years burned down
like a candle!
I will not say: In my life you are the butterfly
but there's not a flicker of a wing,
only that night
washing through
our glittering isolation!

18

سأتحرر من كل شيء:

من عينيكِ اللتين ترقبان غيمة
لن تلد أبداً،
من سطوعك في الحديقة وحيدةً
تنشرين الجنون
على حبل أيامنا الماضية.

من الخسارات الكبيرة
التي أبقت على شيء واحد فقط -
هو هيامي بكِ.

سأتحررُ
من البوح
ومن الصمت أيضاً
فكلاهما يؤدي اليكِ.

لا طريق ثالثاً، إذن،
في هذه المتاهة،

لذلك سأختارُ
النارين معاً!

19

شيء مختلف تماماً
هذا الذي أراه الآن.
شيء له

18

I will unburden myself of everything:

of your eyes, watching a cloud
that will never bring rain;
of your radiance in the garden
as you hang out our foolish past
on the line.

Of the terrible losses
that left me with only one thing—
my love for you.

I will be free
of the revelation
and the silence—
they both only lead to you.

There is no third path
through this labyrinth,

for this reason I will choose
both fires!

19

What I am seeing now
is something entirely different.
Something that combines

بهاء الصمت
والبوح معاً؛
شيء له
قوة الليل
وقوة الشعر؛
لا فضاء محدداً له –
يبتعدُ ثم يقتربُ، يقتربُ ثم يبتعدُ،
هكذا في حلقة مفرغة!

يدعوني اليه.
فارتبك في حضرته.
الغارقة بالنور والظلام
قلت له: كيف جمعت النقيضين؟
قال لي: عندما تكتب البوح
ببهاء الصمت
ستعرف طريقي

واختفى
لا ادري الى أين.

20

عندما كنا معاً تلك الليلة،
لم يكن القمر مضيئاً كعادته
وحتى الأجراس –
الأجراس التي كنا نهتدي بها
أجراس الولادة
أم أجراس الموت
لم تُشِرْ اليكِ.
ولا الى الوردة ورحيقها
الذي انتظر كل تلك السنين.

the majesty of silence
and revelation;
something that holds
the power of darkness
and the power of poetry;
something that occupies no single place—
it's sometimes distant, sometimes close by,
which makes it a vicious cycle!

It calls out to me.
I panic in his presence.
Awash in light and darkness
I said to him, How can you encompass opposites?
He told me: When you write down the revelation
in the magnificence of silence
you will know my way.

And then it disappeared
I've no idea where.

20

That night, when we were together,
the moon didn't shine as normal
and even the bells—
those bells that led us
the bells of birth
or the bells of death
that were not ringing for you,
nor the rose and its sweetness
which has been waiting all these years.

كانت تقرع...

تقرع...

بصمتٍ لا يدانيه شيء.

The bells were ringing . . .
Ringing . . .
in silence.

كتـاب النـسيان

The Book of Oblivion

1

أنا الغياب الذي تجلى في عينيكِ.
أنا بكاؤك الطويل.
أنا معنى أن نكون وحيدين
دونما حتى منفى.

هل قلت العدم
ذلك الذي تحدثنا عنه تلك الليلة
أم كان هناك شيء آخر؟
لا ...
لم يكن الموت؛
الغياب الذي تجلى في عينيكِ
كان أكثر قسوة
من كل ميتاتنا السابقة.

2

أنا وهم.
هذا الذي ترينه أمامكِ
ليس أنا،
ولا هو، بالطبع،
الآخر،
ذلك الذي ضل نسيانه
فأضلته الذاكرة.

إنه الآن
بين ... بين؛
منزلة لا يحسد عليها سواه
في زمن العواصف هذا.

1

I am the absence reflected in your eyes.
I am your endless weeping.
I am what it means to be ourselves alone
without even an exile.

Did I mention the emptiness
we talked about that night,
or was there something else?
No . . .
it was not death;
the absence that shone in your eyes
was more terrible
than all our previous deaths.

2

I am an illusion.
What you see before you
is not me,
nor is it him, obviously,
the other one,
who lost his nonexistence
and in doing so, was lost to memory.

He is now
stuck in
a perilous place
in the stormy season.

3

أنا الليل،
كلّه.
بطوله وعرضه
وسنينه الخاوية.

أنا الوردة قائمة بعكازين.
واحدة لكِ
والأخرى
منفى الكلمة الجديدة
التي تُسمّي الظلامَ ضوءاً
والقيامةَ جسداً
والروحَ وطناً.

تُسمي المدينة البعيدة حلماً
تُهدهده في الانتظار!

4

تمجدُ الريح،
الريح العاصفة التي لا تهدأ،
وتمجد السكون،
السكون المريب الذي لا يهدأ.
تلك المرأة التي تقف وحيدة
في هذا العالم،
لا تهدأ!

تحلم كذلك
بالماضي -
خزانة الألم.
الأيام المسروقة

3

I am the night,
the nothing-but-night.
Its extent and latitude,
its empty years.

I am a rose espaliered between two trellises.
One represents you
and the other
the banishment of a new word
that names the darkness as light
and the resurrection, nothing but a body
And the soul a place to call home.

That word calls the distant city a dream
that calms the word with all its waiting!

4

She sings the praises of the wind,
the hurricane that never subsides.
She is glorifying the stillness,
the uncertain stillness that is never quiet.
Woman, you who stand alone
in this world,
never be at peace!

She also dreams
about the past—
that cupboard where pain is stored.
She dreams about the stolen days,

الذكرى البعيدة.
الجمال الذي لا يهدأ!

5

كيف نحتفلُ
بكل هذا الفرح؟
كيف سنصغي إليه؟

إنه من عالم آخر،
عالم غريب عنا؛
عالم نكون وحيدين فيه
اّلا منكِ،
ومن تلك الوردة التي تلتهب
عندما تراكِ قادمة نحوها.
تحمرُ
كالأمل المنسي
ثم تذوب
ورقة ... ورقة!

6

لا أطمعُ بلهيبكِ أيتها الروح،
ولا أطمع بلهيبكَ أيها الجسد
أطمع فقط
بالمرات القليلة جداً
التي تحدثنا فيها عن الحب
أو حتى عن الموت،
عن رحليك
وأنت تستنشقين أزهار قبلتنا الأولى
البهاء الذي مر كالحلم
والأماني التي ذوت خلفه.

about distant memory.
Such a restless beauty!

5

How can we celebrate
all this joy?
How could we ever hear it?

It comes from another world,
from an alien world,
a world where we can be alone
from everyone but you,
and the flower that bursts into fire
when it sees you approaching.
It blushes
like a forgotten hope,
then withers
leaf by leaf!

6

Soul, I don't crave your flame,
nor do I lust after your flame, my body,
I only long for
those rare times
when we talked of love
or even death,
when we talked of your going away,
smelling the blossoms of our first kiss,
the brilliance that has faded like a dream
and the hopes that withered afterwards.

7

تعالي
هنا الفرحُ كلُّه؛
ارتعاشة القلب
وتصابي الجسد.

تعالي
أيتها الأميرة
وادخلي
ادخلي في معناه،
بنهايته الوحيدة؛
بروحه،
التي غابت كلّ تلك السنين.

ادخلي
في وسامته الضائعة؛
في رسائله الأولى
التي لم يحتفظ بها –
بوهم الكتابة
عنه أو إليه.
فقط ادخلي.
فلن تجدي
بعد حين
سوى السراب.

8

لستُ يوسف.
لم تكن لي فتنته الآسرة
ولم يكن الطريق طويلاً
الى المتاهة

7

Come,
here's all the joy:
the trembling of the heart
and the youthfulness of the body.

Come,
Princess
step into
his senses,
his final destiny,
his soul,
which has been missing for all these years.

Step into
his lost beauty;
step into his first letters
that he burned—
the fantasy of writing
about himself or for himself.
Just step in.
Soon you will find
nothing but a mirage
in there.

8

I am not Joseph.
I never had his charismatic charm
and it was a very short path
to the maze

أو الى البئر
التي لم نشرب منها قطُ
سوى النسيان.

ولم يفقد أبي بصره،
الذي لن يرتد اليه أبداً
مادامت عيناه
تنتظران الضوء!

الظلمة حالكة!
والبئر عميقة
وما من شيء هناك،
لا زليخة
ولا حتى أمل كاذب.

لم يكن أي شيء على الاطلاق،
لقد تكرر علينا القصص.
لكني أعرف
إننا كنا إخوته حقاً.

9

قلتِ:
ستأتي إلينا النهاية
أو سنمضي اليها سراعاً
وليس من عدة لنا -
سوى الكلمات -
وخطايا ارتكبناها معاً،
كانت ضرورية
كي تستقيم الحياة!

or to the well
where we drank nothing
but oblivion.

My father didn't go blind,
but he'll see nothing
so long as his eyes
wait for the light!

The darkness is so filled with dark!
The well so deep
and there's nothing, no one,
no Zulaika
not even one false hope.

Nothing at all.
It was the same story for us.
But I know
we were really his brothers.

9

You said:
The end will come to us
or we will quickly reach the end
and we have nothing—
only words—
and the sins we committed together,
which were so necessary
if we were to live decent lives!

قلتُ:
سنرى الحقيقة أخيراً،
سيغرقنا الدمع
طوفانه الذي لا حد له
والدم...
الدم...
أي نهر سيحتويه؟
وأي أرض سيغرقها
إنه يجري الينا
مسرعاً كالقدر!

قلتُ
وقلتِ
أشياء نرددها
أم ترددنا،
في هذا السجال الطويل
من العدم.

10

أيتها الفتنة الغائبة!
أيها البريق الذي لا ينكسر!
أيها الصدى الذي لا صوت له!
كلمة تُشبه الموت
وتمضي
الى الحقيقة الأخيرة؛
الى القلب؛
ومعناه الخفي؛
الى الدمعة التي يذرفها النسيان،
حقيبة الغياب
وردة المنفى
أو صحراؤه المقيمة فينا.

I said:
Finally we will see the truth;
tears will drown us
in their flood, which has no limit.
And the blood . . .
the blood . . .
which river will be wide enough for it?
Which country will it cover?
The blood flowing towards us
as eagerly as Fate!

I said,
and you said
we repeat things
or things repeat us,
in this long debate
Oblivion holds with itself.

10

O the imaginary spell!
O the gleam that cannot be dulled!
O echo that echoes nothing!
There's only a single word and it sounds like death
then fades
to the final truth,
to the heart,
and its invisible presence,
to the tear oblivion sheds,
to the dismissal of absence,
to the rose of not-belonging
or to the great desert that shifts inside us all.

لا فرق.
كلّ تناله الأزمنة!

11

أنا...
أنا ميت تماماً
هذا الذي ترينه أمامكِ وهم.
ليس له يدان
يحلم بهما.
ولا عينان...

شفتاه تقضي أيامه بالتمائم.
أهواءه الكثيرة المُرّة
يرددها عالياً
في اكتمال النهار.

كلمة خرساء
ـ هو العمر ـ
كالموت
أو النسيان!

12

تغني
وترقص
وحيداً
كغجري
أبكاه الصمت .

It really doesn't matter.
Time will defeat us all!

11

I am . . .
I am quite dead.
This man you see before you is an illusion.
He has no hands
to build his dreams with.
Nor eyes . . .

His lips rehearse magic charms.
He continuously repeats
his many bitter desires
in the shimmer of noon.

Life—
such a silent word—
as is death.
As is oblivion!

12

You sing
and dance
as lonely
as a gypsy whom the silence
has driven to tears.

ترقص...
تغني...
وليس ثمة لك
سوى النسيان،
يغطيك كما الثلج
على أسقف البيوت.
ليس لك فيها سوى روحك
تغني...
ترقص...
وتلهث
نحو الضوء!

You dance
and sing . . .
but there's nothing
to cover you
but oblivion,
as snow covers the roofs.
There is nothing but your soul
singing . . .
dancing . . .
crying out
towards the light!

كتـاب الدمـع

The Book of Tears

1

دعيني أكتب عنكِ قصيدة غزل
سأقول فيها عنكِ:

ليست طويلة تماماً،
وليست لها عينان زرقاوان،
وشعرها لم يكن بلون الذهب
ويداها...
لا أعرف كيف أصفهما...
قلبها فقط
مَن أتاح لي، من دون أن أعرف،
أن أسمو على مدارج النهاية.

2

مَن أنتِ حتى تهدهدي الفجر؟
من انتِ حتى تقولي لا مكان لك
أيها الخوف، لا مكان لك أيها القدر في هذه العتمة
التي يختفي فيها الضوء تماماً
فتساقط الظلمة، كالجبل،
على قلبي؟

3

لستُ وحيداً
في هذه اللعبة؛
لقد كنتِ معي
تتصفحينه كتاب الدمع.

لستُ وحيداً.
لعبة القلق

1

I want you to let me write a ghazal for you
that says,

She's not that tall,
her eyes are anything but blue,
her hair is nothing like the color of gold
and her hands . . . well I don't quite know
how to describe those hands . . .
only her heart, that true compass,
guides me, without knowing,
to climb a staircase to infinity.

2

Woman, who are you to keep the dawn at bay?
Who are you to say there is no place
for fear, or fate in all this dark
where the light vanishes utterly
and that great mountain, the darkness,
weighs down on my heart?

3

This isn't a game
I have played alone:
You have been next to me all the time
leafing through the Book of Tears.

I'm not alone.
The fretful game

كانت حاضرة معنا
في هذا الكتاب
الذي لا يبتدئ ولا ينتهي كالأبد.

4

صمتت سنوات الدمع،
صمت صوته
صمتت فصوله المتعددة.
...
...

لكنكِ مازلت تتحدثين لي بهمس
عن موت الشجرة،
عن الألم الذي يُقيم فيها،
عن حكمة الدمع
فصوله
التي يدونها النسيان.

5

ها أنت تعودين وحيدة
لقد فقدتِ كل شيء تقريباً:

الجذور التي تحدثنا عنها طويلاً
هوياتنا التي يصبغها الألم
الحب ذلك الذي كنا نسوق أقدارنا اليه
كقطيع تائه.

لم نرتو منه يوماً ما.
عطشى...

was always with us
in that same book which, like eternity,
has no beginning and no end.

4

Years of weeping are cloistered now,
no sound of tears falling
through their many seasons.
. . .
. . .

But you still whisper to me
how the tree is dying,
how even now pain lives in it,
how its tears are a sap of understanding
that has many chapters
all written by the nothingness.

5

Then you come back to me alone
almost everything you owned is lost:

    those roots we talked about for such a long time
    our identities delineated by that pain;
    our love, towards which we herd our fates
    as though they were lost sheep.

Love has not quenched us.
We are thirsty . . .

عطشى...
عطشى إليه
ومنه
سراب
يُقيم فينا كالأزل!

6

كلاهما يُدمي القلب
الرحيل إليه أو الرحيل منه
الوطن أو المنفى.

خروجكِ، تلك الليلة أو بقاؤكِ،
عيناكِ اللتان يتلألأ فيهما الدمع
أو المطر الذي تتلألأ خلاله النافذة
غيابكِ وحضوركِ
ليس ثمة فرق
في هذه الصحراء الشاسعة كالروح!

7

لا سكِينةَ لكِ أيتها الروح
يشغلُكِ الحنين
الذي يضلل الذاكرة.

هوجاء
مثل ثور ذبيح،
أو مثل عاصفة ماطرة!

so thirsty . . .
we thirst for love,
we thirst from love
and the mirage love casts
lives inside us forever!

6

Home or exile,
to leave or to remain,
both bleed in the same heart.

Either departing that night or staying home.
Either your eyes, bright with crying,
or sunlit rain, falling beyond the window.
Your presence or your absence,
it doesn't matter which
in that desert as wide as the soul!

7

O soul, there is no rest.
Memory is clouded by the longing
that consumes us.

My soul, you are a whirlwind,
you are a slaughtered bull,
you are rain, falling!

لكنكِ هشة كالأمل،
كالقلق المُرِّ
كليْلة، تحتفين بها، ساهرة.

8

على ظهيرة ذلك الشاطئ البعيد
لم أتحدث عنه
-    الدمع -
مع أهميته لنا.
ولم أتحدث عن الحلم،
أو عن المسرة التي تغيب فيه.

تحدثت فقط عن معجزة
أن نكون معاً.

- حضورُكِ -
الذي رقصناه
ونحن نسبح في مجد الرغبة العظيمة.
رغبة كانت تتسلقنا، هي،
لا نحن،
كضجة عارمة.

9

يا لأرواحي المتقاتلة
يا لهذا النور وهذا الظلام
أيهما سينطفئ أولاً؟
كيف أنجو، متى ستحدث المعجزة
وينهار جبل الثلج؟

But you break as easily as hope,
as bitter as regret,
as a night celebrating the dawn.

8

Noon. On that far shore
I never mentioned
—the tears—
although it was important for us.
I didn't talk about the dream either,
or the joy that vanished with it.

All I could talk about was the miracle
of us together.

We danced
—your presence—
while we threw ourselves into desire.
It was desire that mounted us;
we did not mount desire.
It was an unconquerable emotion.

9

Oh my souls, always battling
the light against the dark,
which one of you will die first?
What miracle could let me live through
the iceberg foundering?

متاهة كبيرة هذه الأبدية
لا الشمس
ولا البحر
ولا الكلمات
كفيلة بهزيمتها.

فدعها تمر
لا تكبلها بالدمع
دعها تمر كما لو أن لا شيء يحدث.

10

لم أسمع ذلك الصوت،
لم أتبين كلماته المتقطعة،
الانكسار الذي فيه؛
ألم الغياب
أيقونته في الصدى.

لم أسمع أي شيء
فقط: وداعاً
ليختفي الصوت
والانكسار الذي فيه
بينما الصدى ظل حائراً
يردد أنغامه في المدى!

11

لا تعني شيئاً هذه التواريخ
سوى أنها كانت في يوم ما
ملاذاً للدمع،

Eternity is an infinite maze
not sun,
sea,
or words
can overwhelm it.

So let it be,
don't bother trying to shackle it with tears
Let it go as if nothing had happened.

10

I heard no voice,
no occasional words,
the echo that exists in it;
the pain of absence
and its image inside that echo.

I heard nothing
but "Good-bye"
then the voice fell silent
and the distortion
while the baffled echo was
reuttering its descants in the void.

11

Dates mean nothing to me at all
other than that one day.
Dates were nothing but places where sadness lived safe,

ووحشته التي تكفّلتْ بالعمر،
مثل روزنامة بالية.

فكيف سأكتب عنها؟
كيف أدون الحلم
الذي تلاشى فيها؟
الأمنيات الكثيرة الناقصة
ألبوم الدمع
الذي تحفره الذاكرة!

12

هل ستكتب عن الفرح؟
ربما،
وسأكتب عن غنائه
عن الآمال المتجددة فيه.

وماذا عن مسراتكَ الذابلة؟
لا فرق عندي الآن
عادت أم لم تعد.

فالعتمة تبدو لي أحياناً
فيضاً من نور
أحلق فيه دونما أجنحة
أو سماء.

13

أنا وأنتِ والفتنة -
معادلة طالما حلمتُ بها،
فلماذا أخاف اقترابكِ

where time's dark moments,
like the calendar itself, rotted away.

How could I ever write about them?
How could I write down the dream
that I lost with them?
How could I write down all those stillborn hopes
the catalogue of tears
that memory wrote?

12

Will you write about joy?
Perhaps.
And I'll write about its songs
about the hopes it keeps alive.

And what about your faded pleasures?
It makes no difference to me now
whether they come back or not.

Sometimes the darkness seems to me
an ocean built from light
and I'm flying through it with no need for wings,
with no need for sky.

13

The two of us and the spell—
that's an equation I always dreamed of,
so why was I so afraid as you drew near

أيتها المرأة
التي تُشبه النار
والقيامة
التي تُشبه الجسد
يقف هائماً
كالفراشة يحترق، يحترق
مستجيراً
كعادته
من لظى الروح
بلظى الجسد!

14

كيف سأكتب عنها؟
تلك التي سحرت الملائكة والشياطين معاً.
سأكتب، ربما، عن زهوها،
لكن خوفها؛
وحدتها الطويلة
خلف الدمع.
كيف سأكتب عنها؟
وعن النور الذي سرقته العتمة؟
وعن الجنون، الأنيس القديم،
ظل يرفرف عالياً
كأيامها الماضية
كيف وكيف؟
لا إجابة هناك سوى الدمع.

15

هذا الخسران له أوجه متعددة.
لس الفراغ

woman
who thinks fire
is a form of resurrection
just as the body
when it stands consumed
like a flame-scorched butterfly
as ever
to protect itself by fleeing
from the fire of soul
to the fire of body!

14

How can I write about her?
She could charm angels and devils.
I'll tell the world, perhaps, how haughty she was,
but her fearfulness
of being alone forever
and the loneliness behind those tears
how will I write about that?
And about the light in her, consumed by darkness?
Our old friend, madness,
still soaring above
as in her days of old.
How can I?
Tears are the only answer.

15

This loss has many faces.
The emptiness won't satisfy him,

ولا آثار الحب
ولا أوتار القلب تكفيه!

فالأمل الذي أرى صورته
من بعيد
ثمل الآن
مع البراءة التي اختفت
والأحلام التي اختفت
بملامح الوجه القديم
بالعزلة التي تحيط بنا.

16

المقهى هو هو
الموسيقى هي هي
النافذة
الطاولات
عاملة المقهى
منفضة السجائر الوحيدة في الخارج
كل شيْ مثل كل شيء.

مع ذلك لم تكن هي
كان ثمة شيء منها يطوف في المكان
الذي كان هو هو ، في زمان لم يكن هو هو .
ما هذا؟!
لا أعرف!

nor the workings of love,
nor the tuned strings of the heart!

The hope that I may see its image
from afar
is lost now
with the lost innocence
and the evaporated dreams,
by age inscribing its name in the face
and the loneliness that surrounds us.

16

The cafe hadn't changed at all:
the same music,
the same window,
the same tables,
the same waitress.
Even that same ashtray set outside the door.
Everything still looked exactly like everything.

But she was no longer she
and something of her haunted that restless place,
that identical place, but locked in a different time.
And what or when or where it was—
who knows?

متاهة

Labyrinth

لا تقف...
لا تقف
عند منتصف العمر.

اكمله،
ذلك النهار اليتيم.

اقترب منها
المتاهة.

ضع يدك عليها؛
تلمسها.
سترى الجمر
خلف تلك البرودة الظاهرة،
أو سترى الدمعة.

أو ربما لن ترى شيئاً
يستحق ذكره في هذه القصيدة.

Don't stop . . .
Don't stop . . .
at life's center.

Finish it,
this orphaned day.

Draw close
to the maze.

And lay your hands on it;
touch it.
You may see embers glowing
beneath the appearance of cold,
or you may find tears.

Or perhaps you'll find nothing
worth the telling, in this poem.

Ghareeb Iskander is an Iraqi poet living in London. He has published several books including *High Darkness*, *A Chariot of Illusion*, *Translating Sayyab into English* and *For No One's Sake*. He was the featured writer of Scottish Pen 2014.

John Glenday is the author of four collections of poetry; *Grain* (2009) was shortlisted for the Griffin International Poetry Prize. His most recent, *The Golden Mean*, was published in September 2015.